47

A Transformational Journal

Lessons that create passion, love, vitality and abundance.

Dr. E. Jaye Johnson

Elev8ed Guru Publishing

Burbank, California

First paperback edition April 2021.

Edited by Patti Dershem
Cover art by Purple Label Consulting

www.47Journal.com
www.drejayejohnson.com

Elev8ed Guru Publishing
827 North Hollywood Way, Suite 156
Burbank, California 91505

www.elev8edguru.com

I dedicate this book to

Arlena V. Chandler
&
Patricia A. Dershem

Thank you both for being shining examples of Love in its purest form.

Introduction

Hi there! I am excited that our paths have crossed and grateful you chose to pick up this book.

Let me start by sharing that this book was created just for you. Yes, you! I believe that the idea to create this book began with the fact that someone (consciously or unconsciously) asked for it. This started causing a series of amazing cosmic and energetic events to occur such that the idea could be gifted to me and here we are. So, thank you for asking for it and away we go!

Every year around my birthday I start to reflect on lessons learned, goals, and my purpose here. It has become a tradition to sit down and get still and really take a discerning look at my life as a birthday ritual. Do you have a birthday ritual? If I am being honest, birthdays in themselves are rituals. I notice how mine have changed over the years. As a kid they included cakes, parties, and play. As a teen they included cakes, parties, and play. In my twenties they included cakes, parties, cocktails and play. In my thirties they still included cakes, parties, even more cocktails and... play. Now, well into my forties, they include reflection, retrospection, spiritual exploration, reverse gifting (when you give to others in honor of your birthday) and still a bit of play. I am adding a new one this year at 47, publishing a book. The amazing discovery there is when celebrating now, is having the opportunity to highlight the amazing life I've lived and to express gratitude for all the lessons that showed up on my path.

The whole purpose of this book is to share the most impactful lessons that I've discovered, 47 of them to be exact. All 47 have made it possible for me to live an extraordinary life filled with love, prosperity, abundance and peace and I'm not saying that I've never faced challenges or that I haven't had areas of pain. I am saying that if I am really honest, so far these 47 years on the planet have presented bumpy roads, amazing rooms, and so many roads of transformation and self-discovery. So take these 47 lessons and utilize them in your experience.

It is my hope that they bring you an opportunity that allows you to create a life that you absolutely enjoy waking up to every single day. I know, as I look back and apply these principles to my life over and over again, it offers me an opportunity to wake up every day with a smile on my face, complete gratitude in my heart and a way to continue to strive, grow and stretch. Don't get me wrong, I am not claiming to know it all. There are wiser ones on this planet walking with us. I'm just here to cause you to think just a little bit outside of the box and if you do read this book the way it suggests, I would wish for you to take every one of the lessons and focus on it for one week and discover what emerges out of that. I guarantee you'll see results that you didn't even think were possible, you'll have experiences that you weren't even thinking were available and you'll create relationships that will be deep and rich and filled with love.

How to best take this book on.

This is part education, part personal development, part self-discovery, part science project, and part experimental. Just experiment taking this on and doing this book the way it feels best for you. I'm here to offer you only a sample of what you might do that might bring about the great results that I know each one of these principles will offer. However, if you have your own practice, your own ritual, all that I ask is that you incorporate this into what you already do and then note the results, note the magic, note the miracles that manifest as a result. So, here are your instructions or your mission should you choose to proudly accept it.

Walk through this book one week at a time for the next 47 weeks. All you need to do is read the principle or lesson that's there and take it into your practice. Make a commitment to do your very best to stay in alignment with that lesson for an entire week. Focus on it, read it daily, check in with yourself and see how you're doing. That's all you need to do, discover what there is to notice -- if things show up differently in the world, if people show up differently than they ever have before, take note of that. Write it down here so that you can gauge where things are emerging and maybe life is showing up differently for you. It's as simple as that. Step one -- read one lesson per week, take it into whatever spiritual practice you have, pray with it as an intention of how you'd like to show up in the world, meditate on it, take it into your DNA and then review it every single day for a week. Step two -- Focus your energy on your actions to be in alignment with that principle every single day. Step three -- Journal about the process. Write, sketch, illustrate your insights and actions on the page of this journal. The bottom line is you've got this. I know that if you want to live an extraordinary life, it's all available to you inside of these 47 lessons. So I thank you for being courageous and stepping into this mission. I know that you'll be an amazing example of what each one of these lessons represents and I know that you will share that with your world who will then share it with a greater world.

Let's get started.

1.

Love Has No Conditions

Anything with conditions isn't truly love.

This week's practice is loving without preferences, conditions or expectations.
Just love everything and everyone.

Insights:

Actions:

2.

Embrace Transformation

It can be scary and unsettling, yet, so worth going on the ride.

Push yourself to grow and transform things in all areas of your life. Break the status quo.

Insights:

Actions:

3.

Lessons Will Repeat

Life lessons repeat themselves until we get them. They get bigger and even more dramatic/traumatic with every repeat.

Take some time to reflect and discover some moments where lessons presented themselves and maybe you didn't take heed and they showed up again. Patterns are fertile ground for overlooked lessons.

Insights:

Actions:

4.

Integrity

Let integrity guide your words and actions.

Do what you say you will do when you say you will do it. Do the right thing even when no one is looking.

Insights:

Actions:

5.

Embrace Your Power

You have only scratched the surface of how powerful you are.

This week acknowledge and embrace the power that resides in you. Dig deep and step into your power.

Insights:

Actions:

6.

Master Energy

Everything is energy. Gain mastery in managing yours.

Pay attention to what gives you energy and what you give your energy to. Look for that which leaves you feeling energy-depleted and deal with it.

Insights:

Actions:

7.

Front Row Tickets

Everyone doesn't need to have a front row seat in your life. Some people you get to love from afar.

Look for those relationships that drain your energy and don't celebrate you. Sometimes you have to create distance.

Insights:

Actions:

8.

Be Responsible

Power comes from taking responsibility for **everything** in your life.

There is freedom in taking responsibility for everything in your life. Look for areas in your life where you have become passive or maybe even a victim.

Insights:

Actions:

9.

Not Your Business

What people think of you is **none of your business**.

This is huge, concerning yourself with what people think of you will keep you distracted forever.

This week examine how much other people's thoughts about you make an impact on how you live your life.

Insights:

Actions:

10.

Expansion Required

If you are not growing, learning and expanding, you are killing yourself slowly.
Everything and everyone must expand.

How can you grow and stretch yourself? Find ways in which you are already
doing this and create new ways as well.

Insights:

Actions:

11.

R.I.S.K. It All

Relentless Inspired Spiritual Knowing. With RISK there is great reward. Boldly follow your heart and your dreams.

Find opportunities to take a greater RISK and do it.

Insights:

Actions:

12.

Challenges/Traumas/Hardships = Something Badass Is Emerging

Just on the other side of the challenge is greatness and opportunity. Stay focused on what is trying to emerge from the challenge.

As you face a challenge/trauma/hardship this week get present to what is awaiting you on the other side of it.

Insights:

Actions:

13.

FAIL Forward Fast

There are great lessons to be discovered in the failures, embrace them.

Take actions this week that you have been holding off because you think it will
fail and record your discoveries.

Insights:

Actions:

14.

Celebrate All Wins

Celebrate the wins of others even when you desire what they have.

Create opportunities to genuinely celebrate another person's success without comparing yourself and wishing it had happened to you.

Insights:

Actions:

15.

Breathe

Every breath is a new opportunity to **return to love, return to peace, start anew.**

Practice breathing this week, intentional breathing. Take a moment and just breathe. What comes to mind during this intentional breathing?

Insights:

Actions:

16.

Heart Centered

Lead with your heart.

Take this week and speak, do, share everything from your heart. What miracles show up?

Insights:

Actions:

17.

Give It Away

What you desire most, give it away.

Give to others what you want most. If you want people to listen to you, listen to others with complete attention. Want love? Give more love then you ever have before.

Insights:

Actions:

18.

Character Evaluation

Who are you when no one is looking?

Reflect on who you are when no one is looking. Do you like yourself? Do you love yourself? Write yourself a love letter. Acknowledge your amazingness and superpowers, note areas for growth.

Insights:

Actions:

19.

Intuition

Trust your intuition. Listen and trust yourself.

Practice trusting your intuition this week. Don't question it, just trust it.

Insights:

Actions:

20.

Lack Is Not Real

There is never a lack of anything ever, only a misalignment with it manifesting.

In what areas in your life do you feel there is a sense of lack? Explore your thoughts around this. Look for ways to create thoughts of abundance in these areas.

Insights:

Actions:

21.

Teach

We teach well what we most need to learn and master.

Spend some time this week sharing your knowledge with others.

Insights:

Actions:

22.

Authentically Be

Always show up as who you are authentically and never ever apologize for it.

Look for ways to share who you are with even more authenticity.

Insights:

Actions:

23.

Build People Up

Build people up. Love, acknowledge, support, edify and listen to people. It costs you nothing.

Go all out and boldly build people up this week in a loving and authentic way.

Insights:

Actions:

24.

See Yourself In Everyone

See what connects us all. Oneness.

Treat everyone as if they are you. Connect with what unites us all.

Insights:

Actions:

25.

No Separation

There is no separation between you and the Source that created it ALL.

Sit in stillness and listen to it. Note your findings. Practice daily. Even take one question into the stillness and listen.

Insights:

Actions:

26.

Forgiveness

Forgiveness doesn't condone, it releases.

Practice random acts of forgiveness, let go of old stuff.

Insights:

Actions:

27.

Choose Your Adventure

Protect your perspective. Be discerning when being influenced.

Play with changing your perspective this week. Stretch to look at things through new lenses.

Insights:

Actions:

28.

Present

Be here **NOW.**

Give it your all to stay in every moment. Note when you think back into the past
or look ahead into the future and bring yourself back to the moment at hand.

Insights:

Actions:

29.
Share The Love
Make sure that the ones you love know you love them, not just by saying it but by your actions.

Demonstrate your love to the people in your life this week.

Insights:

Actions:

30.

Why Ask Why

Asking "why" questions gets you useless answers and puts you on a rollercoaster of judgement.

Dig in this week and take note of when you are asking "why" questions. What information do you get? Do you then judge the answer?

Insights:

Actions:

31.

Paddle, Paddle

If life feels like you are paddling upstream, you need to turn your "boat" around. Forcing something to work never turns out well.

Spend the week turning your "boat" around. When the energy around failed attempts feels frenetic or chaotic, this is evidence of paddling upstream. Discover ways to be in the flow.

Insights:

Actions:

32.

How Can I?

Asking "how" questions gets you to solutions.

Take this week to explore life from the perspective of "how can I?."

Insights:

Actions:

33.

Self-Care

Self-care isn't optional, it is a mandate.

How can you incorporate self-care into your life on a regular basis? How can you make it a priority?

Insights:

Actions:

34.

My Rooms

If you are always the smartest or wealthiest person in the room, you are in the wrong room.

Create opportunities to be challenged and learn from others. Strike up friendships with people who know what you want to know and have what you desire.

Insights:

Actions:

35.

Wonder

Approach everything with childlike wonder and playfulness.

Discover ways to bring childlike wonder and playfulness into your life this week.
Let go of being so serious and see what happens.

Insights:

Actions:

36.

Brand New

Experience everything newly. Even if you have done it a million times.

Take on doing everything as if it were for the first time, like a brand new experience.

Insights:

Actions:

37.

Curiosity

Be curious about life.

Make a point to be curious this week. Do things you've never done before. Do
things you have done before, only do them differently.

Insights:

Actions:

38.
Like v Love
Like is conditional. Love isn't.

Where have you placed conditions and called it love?

Insights:

Actions:

39.

People v Actions

People are not their actions. Actions are filtered through what is happening and
various circumstances.

How often do you judge people based on their actions? Where have you
applied a label to someone based upon a single action?

Insights:

Actions:

40.

Cloudy Future

Taking your past into your future clouds it and conceals the light.

Note when you base what is happening in the present moment on something from the past -- or when you compare past experiences to the present and even use them as a prediction of what will happen in the future.

Insights:

Actions:

41.

Stillness

Be still. Get quiet. Listen. The answers are in the stillness.

Use this week to practice stillness and listening.

Insights:

Actions:

42.
Be The Leader
A great leader has mastered the art of following.

Look for areas in your life where you can step up and lead more and areas where you can empower others to lead and follow more.

Insights:

Actions:

43.

State of Emotions

Master your emotions. You get to choose your emotional state. Never let something or someone steal your joy.

Practice staying present. Practice not allowing external circumstances to impact your emotional state of choice. If it is joy, let nothing separate you from fundamental joy. That is not to say don't feel or have empathy, just choose instead of being dragged into a state you don't want to be in.

Insights:

Actions:

44.
Gratitude
Be grateful, period.

Find and acknowledge everything there is to be grateful for.

Insights:

Actions:

45.

Be A Contribution

Give from your heart, your skills, you gifts, your talents. Share yourself.

Be a solution this week. Share ideas, support people. Be a cheerful giver.

Insights:

Actions:

46.

Greater Expression

EVERYTHING is ALWAYS working towards and lining up for a greater expression of you to emerge.

This week step into the power and magnificence that you are. Explore opportunities to be the light in the darkness, be kind, be wisdom, be the example.

Insights:

Actions:

47.

Agility

Flexibility and agility keep you present and open for the miraculous.

For our final week of practice be open to the possibility that everything can change in an instant. Pivot quickly, be open to new possibilities.

Insights:

Actions:

Thank you for taking this journey with me. It is my hope that you have discovered many new things about yourself and others. Keep challenging yourself and pushing yourself to expand and I promise you will continue to not just live but thrive.

Please share your experiences with me. You can post on social media with the hashtag #47lessons. You can join the community Facebook Group 47 Lessons where I share other insights. You can follow me on all social media platforms @drejayejohnson. Or download free content at my website www.drejayejohnson.com or visit www.47journal.com

Love and Light,
E. Jaye

www.ingramcontent.com/pod-product-compliance
Lightning Source LLC
Chambersburg PA
CBHW061159040426
42445CB00013B/1739